AF483125

Josie and Doug

An Adventure with The Loveland Frogman

Written by Mike Meldon

Illustrated by Rachel Royer

ISBN: #9798330266296
Library of Congress Control Number: #2024913719

Written By Mike Meldon
Consultant/Editor: Doug Gilbert
Illustrations and Cover Design: Rachel Royer

To the People of Loveland, Ohio that keep the positive spirit
of the Loveland Frogman alive with all that they do for our city
and for one another.

In the town of Loveland, where the Little Miami flows,

Lived Josie and Doug, two friends you may know.

The Official Frogman Search Team was gathered,

Under the golden moonlight.

"We're going on a mission:

To find the Loveland Frogman tonight."

PAXTON'S GRILL
LOVE OUR LAND
LOVE OUR LAND
LOVELAND FROGMAN
LOVE OUR LAND

Legend in Loveland had it, that hidden around there,

Lived a **mysterious cryptid** that caused many some fear.

Some said it was a magical being,

While others thought it was fake.

But Josie, Doug and team were ready

To search the river, woods, and lakes.

LOVELAND'S LEGENDARY
FROGMAN
REAL OR FAKE? FRIEND OR FOE?
JOIN OUR TEAM FOR THE SEARCH!
MEET 12PM AT PAXTONS!
PAXTON'S GRILL
BRING YOUR FLASHLIGHT!
josie

So the team wandered out with the moon lighting their way,
To search for the Frogman without delay.
The quest had just started and the creature was out!
He turned to greet them with a friendly smile and loud shout.

"Hello all! I've been waiting for you, all through the night!
Come and sit with me here, there is no need for fright."
With his wise eyes, long legs and high back lump,
The Frogman welcomed them into his secret home, inside a tree stump.

He explained that he lived out in the woods—stays hidden and afar,
To keep watch and protect the species that needed his guard.
They were **vulnerable**, **threatened**, **endangered** or labeled 'of concern'.
Those words meant they were in trouble—he wanted the team to learn.

ENDANGERED SPECIES
Fly Recipes
OHIO NATIVE PLANTS
Legends of Ohio
THE HISTORY OF LOVELAND
BIRDS OF OHIO
Loveland Castle
REPTILES OF OHIO
OHIO WETLANDS
LOVE OUR LAND
LOVE OUR LAND

The old Frogman led Josie, Doug, and the rest of the team
Through both days and night—it felt like a dream.
There were bees, birds, fish, and **mammals** that needed help and aid.
Along with **amphibians** and **reptiles** that needed help being saved.

In the meadows and fields, where wildflowers sway,

The Frogman guided them along the way.

Among the blooms, with a buzz so sweet,

They found an **American Bumblebee**, buzzing at their feet.

But the Frogman shared, with a sad tone,

The **American Bumblebee** struggles, its habitat is almost gone

It's hard to find pollen, and **insecticides** make them ill

"This bee is special," the Frogman says, "it needs our help."

He asks if they will.

In the reedy marshes, where the tall grasses sway,
The Loveland Frogman led them, they all made their way.
Amongst the cattails, in a stance so grand,
They glimpsed the **American Bittern**, a bird so rare in the land.

But the Frogman shared, with a serious tale,
"The beautiful bittern was endangered as well.
It's losing the habitat, where it makes its nest,
We need to save the grasses and cattails, that will be best."

The Loveland Frogman led them, in the gentle currents of the river's flow,
They spotted the **River Darter**, a fish you should know.
With its sleek form and fins that gleam,
It darted and swirled, it swam like a dream.

But the Frogman spoke, he had more bad news,
"The rivers are polluted, the ones that they use.
Respect its waters, we need to keep the **River Darter**'s habitats clean,
Because this endangered species is seldom seen."

High up in a snag, in the deep forest dark and black,
The Frogman took them, to an **Indiana Bat**.
It eats moths and bugs, this creature of the night.
To see a flying mammal is a truly special sight.

But the Frogman shared, with a pitiful sigh,
"The **Indiana Bats** are now rare to find.
Respect its roosts, and the insects it eats at night.
Let's all work together to get this right."

LOVE OUR LAND
LOVE OUR LAND
PROTECT THE BATS — STAY OUT
CAVE CLOSED — DO NOT ENTE
PROTECT THE BATS — STAY OU

Then in the forest he showed them, where leaves softly lie,
The **Spotted Salamander**, a creature of the night.
With their chunky body and big yellow dots,
They crawled through moss in search of wet spots.

But the Frogman spoke, with a heavy heart,
Of the **Spotted Salamander**, endangered in part.
"Her habitat — rare vernal pools — is under attack.
They are in trouble and need our help to fight back."

LOVE
OUR
LAND
LOVE OUR
Josie

And again, in the woodland's embrace where the trees stand tall,
The Loveland Frogman introduced them to the Woodland Box Turtle.
With its sturdy shell and eyes so wise,
It wandered the forest, under the leaves and skies.

But the Frogman shared, with a serious tone,
"The Woodland Box Turtle, they are often alone.
Respect its habitat, its home in the wood,
And help them cross the streets while in your neighborhood."

STOP
TURTLE CROSSING
STOP
LOVE the LAND

As Doug, Josie and the team

Had finished their long tour,

They had learned a lot, for sure.

LoveLand
Love the LAND

They promised to help their new friend, The Frogman,
In the creeks, meadows, neighborhoods, and forests of Loveland,
And protect nature's creatures big and small.
Especially those that need our help most of all.

LOVELAND FROGMAN
SEARCH TEAM
LOVE OUR LAND
BELIEVE.
LOVE OUR LAND

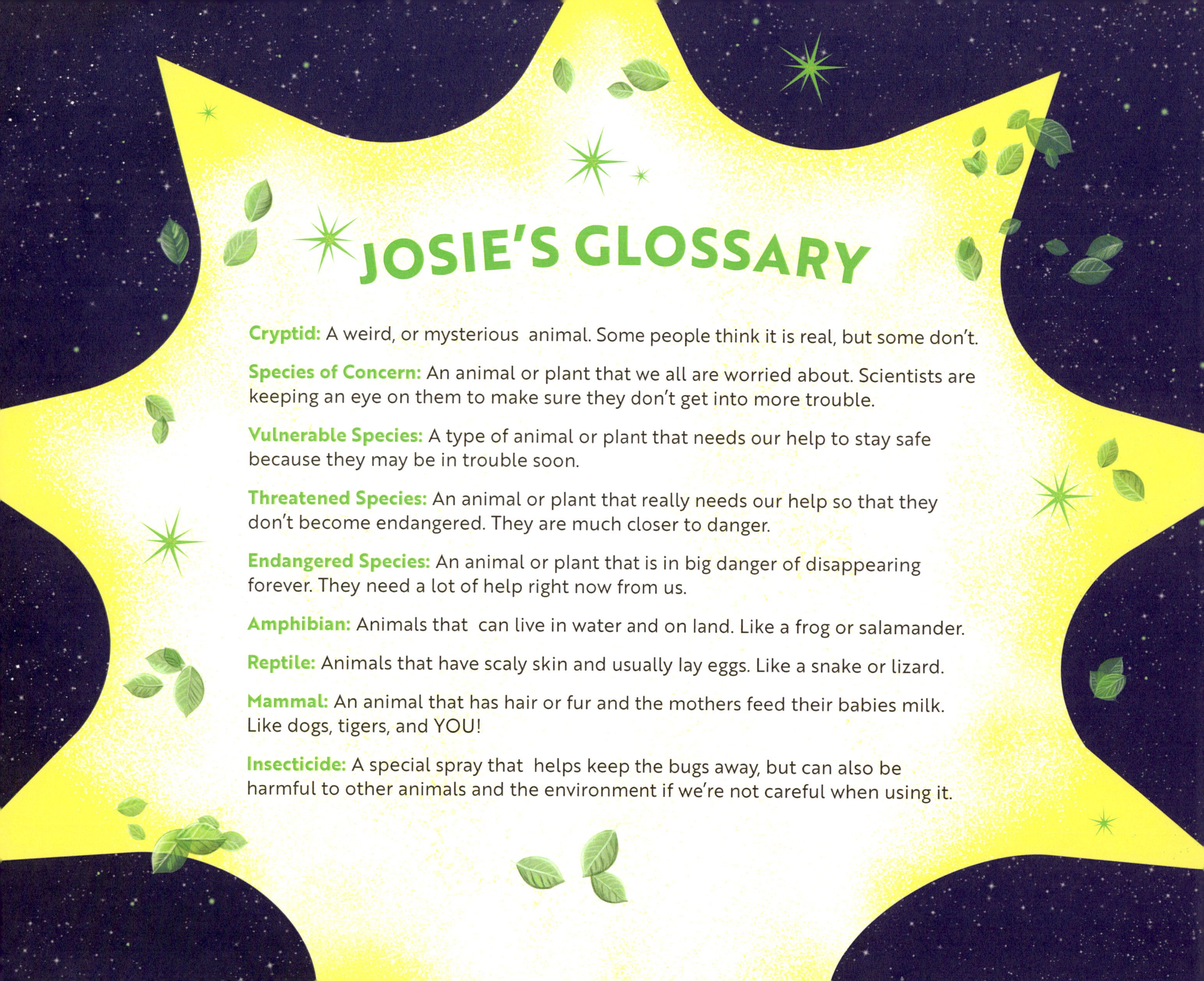

JOSIE'S GLOSSARY

Cryptid: A weird, or mysterious animal. Some people think it is real, but some don't.

Species of Concern: An animal or plant that we all are worried about. Scientists are keeping an eye on them to make sure they don't get into more trouble.

Vulnerable Species: A type of animal or plant that needs our help to stay safe because they may be in trouble soon.

Threatened Species: An animal or plant that really needs our help so that they don't become endangered. They are much closer to danger.

Endangered Species: An animal or plant that is in big danger of disappearing forever. They need a lot of help right now from us.

Amphibian: Animals that can live in water and on land. Like a frog or salamander.

Reptile: Animals that have scaly skin and usually lay eggs. Like a snake or lizard.

Mammal: An animal that has hair or fur and the mothers feed their babies milk. Like dogs, tigers, and YOU!

Insecticide: A special spray that helps keep the bugs away, but can also be harmful to other animals and the environment if we're not careful when using it.

MEET THE REAL
DOUG & JOSIE